ACTION GAMES

BY JULIANNA HELT

Apex is distributed by North Star Editions:
sales@northstareditions.com | 888-417-0195

Produced for Apex by Red Line Editorial.

Photographs ©: Shutterstock Images, cover, 1, 4–5, 6–7, 8, 9, 12, 13, 14–15, 16–17, 18, 19, 20–21, 22–23, 24–25, 26, 26–27, 29; iStockphoto, 10–11

Library of Congress Control Number: 2022920699

ISBN
978-1-63738-571-5 (hardcover)
978-1-63738-625-5 (paperback)
978-1-63738-727-6 (ebook pdf)
978-1-63738-679-8 (hosted ebook)

Printed in the United States of America
Mankato, MN
082023

NOTE TO PARENTS AND EDUCATORS

Apex books are designed to build literacy skills in striving readers. Exciting, high-interest content attracts and holds readers' attention. The text is carefully leveled to allow students to achieve success quickly. Additional features, such as bolded glossary words for difficult terms, help build comprehension.

TABLE OF CONTENTS

CHAPTER 1

RUN, JUMP, PLAY

A boy grips a video game controller. His **character** runs across the screen. The boy taps a button, and his character jumps. He bumps into coins to collect them.

Some video game controllers use cords to send signals. Others are wireless.

But the boy must watch out.
Monsters run along the ground.
The boy is careful not to hit
them. His character must also
jump over holes.

Platform games often have flat, or 2D, art.

PLATFORM GAMES

In platform games, characters run and jump on flat ledges. They also dodge **obstacles**. In some games, the ground moves, too. Players must run to avoid falling off.

In the *Mario* games, players move through levels to complete them.

The boy reaches the end of the first level. In level two, there are more monsters. The boy works harder to dodge them.

In games like *Crash Bandicoot*, players must complete dozens of levels to win.

FAST FACT

Only some action games have levels. Others last until a character dies.

CHAPTER 2

ABOUT ACTION GAMES

Action games are about **physical** challenges. Players may shoot or solve puzzles. They also run and jump.

In *Donkey Kong*, players move up and down ladders.

The first action games were arcade games. To play, people put coins into machines that looked like boxes. They used buttons or **joysticks** as controls.

Malls and restaurants often had arcade games for people to play.

Pac-Man first came out in 1980.

FAST FACT

Pac-Man was a popular arcade game. Players moved through a maze. They tried to eat dots and avoid ghosts.

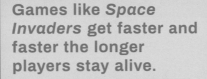

Games like *Space Invaders* get faster and faster the longer players stay alive.

Action games often have levels. To pass each level, players must think and move quickly. Sometimes, they must fight **bosses**.

SPACE INVADERS

Space Invaders was one of the first action video games. It was invented in 1978 in Japan. Players shot aliens. The aliens dropped from the top of the screen.

CHAPTER 3

SHOOT, FIGHT, HIDE

There are many types of action games. Each type has different goals. In platform games, players try to move safely through each level. They also collect **items** to score points.

People can play action games on consoles, computers, or smartphones.

In shooter and fighting games, the goal is to beat enemies. Shooter games focus on weapons. In fighting games, characters kick or punch.

In first-person shooter games, the player sees from the character's point of view.

In third-person games like *Street Fighter*, players see their characters from above or the side.

STREET FIGHTER

Street Fighter II is a famous fighting game. Players fight each other one-on-one. They press a series of buttons to do special moves.

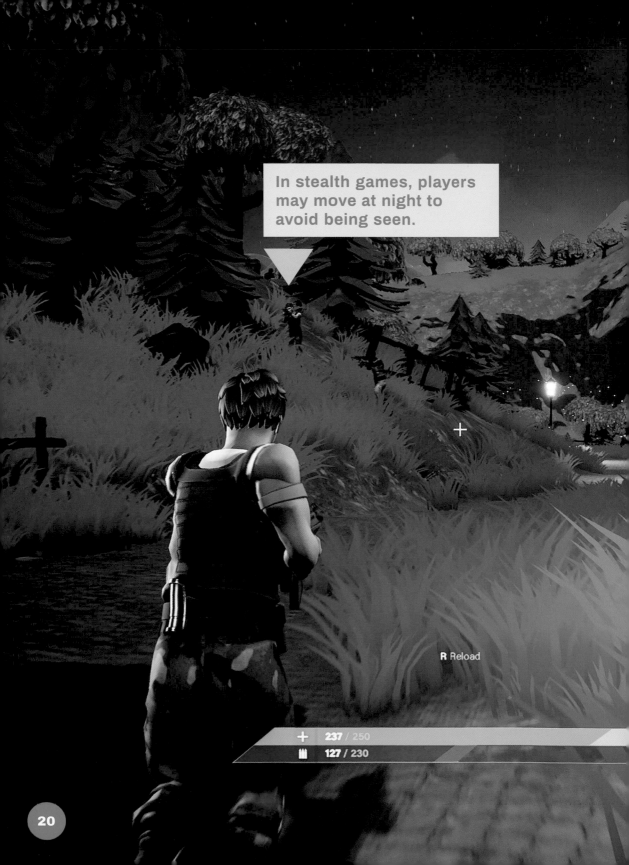

In stealth games, players may move at night to avoid being seen.

R Reload

237 / 250
127 / 230

In stealth games, players must sneak around. They try not to be seen by other characters. Players hide or make surprise attacks.

FAST FACT

Assassin's Creed is a stealth game. It is based on events from the past.

CHAPTER 4

EVEN MORE OPTIONS

Survival games are another type of action game. Players try to stay alive. They may fight. But they also build and collect **resources**.

Minecraft is one example of a survival game.
Players build and explore in a world made of cubes.

People can play *Fortnite* online for free.

Battle royale games are a type of survival game. Many players fight one another. The last player alive wins.

FAST FACT

Popular battle royale games include Fortnite and Call of Duty: Warzone.

Each game in the *Legend of Zelda* series tells part of a story.

THE LEGEND OF ZELDA

The Legend of Zelda is a series of action-adventure games. It follows a boy named Link. Link must save a princess named Zelda. Together, they must fight an evil villain.

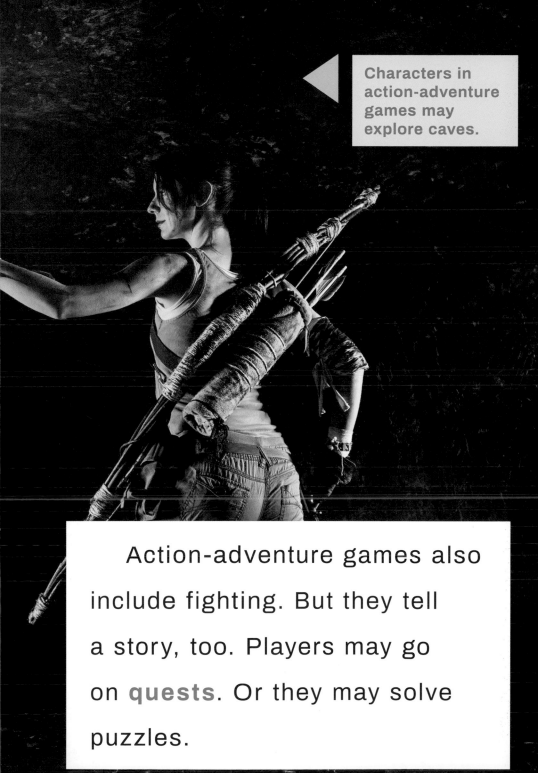

Characters in action-adventure games may explore caves.

Action-adventure games also include fighting. But they tell a story, too. Players may go on **quests**. Or they may solve puzzles.

COMPREHENSION QUESTIONS

Write your answers on a separate piece of paper.

1. Write a sentence that explains one thing all action games have in common.

2. Would you rather play a survival game or a stealth game? Why?

3. What is the goal of a battle royale game?

   A. to jump over obstacles
   B. to be the last player alive
   C. to go on a quest

4. What is one goal players have in a platform game?

   A. to fall off ledges
   B. to crash into monsters
   C. to avoid monsters

5. What does **stealth** mean in this book?

*In **stealth** games, players must sneak around. They try not to be seen by other characters.*

    A. being loud and strong
    B. staying hidden
    C. holding still

6. What does **villain** mean in this book?

*Link must save a princess named Zelda. Together, they must fight an evil **villain**.*

    A. a good guy
    B. a bad guy
    C. a place on a map

Answer key on page 32.

GLOSSARY

bosses
Extra-strong enemies that players must defeat to finish a quest or level.

character
A person in a book, movie, or video game.

items
Objects, such as coins, that characters can get in video games.

joysticks
Sticks that people tilt and turn to control a video game.

obstacles
Things that block the way.

physical
Involving speed, strength, or quick movements.

quests
Long or hard journeys to find objects or complete tasks.

resources
Important supplies such as food, money, or building materials.

TO LEARN MORE

BOOKS

Abdo, Kenny. *Fortnite*. Minneapolis: Abdo Publishing, 2022.

Duling, Kaitlyn. *Level Up: Secrets of the Games We Love*.
  Vero Beach, FL: Rourke Educational Media, 2021.

Tulien, Sean. *Video Games: A Graphic History*. Minneapolis:
  Lerner Publishing, 2021.

ONLINE RESOURCES

Visit **www.apexeditions.com** to find links and resources
related to this title.

ABOUT THE AUTHOR

Julianna Helt is a former children's librarian turned children's
book author. She enjoys researching and writing about all
sorts of topics. She lives in Pittsburgh with her husband, two
teenagers, and three cats.

INDEX

ANSWER KEY:
1. Answers will vary; 2. Answers will vary; 3. B; 4. C; 5. B; 6. B